Men and Beasts

Themes

Men and Beasts

Imagination

Conflict

Generations

A Teacher's Book accompanies each volume

Men and Beasts

edited by Rhodri Jones

**Heinemann Educational
Books Ltd: London**

Heinemann Educational Books Ltd

LONDON EDINBURGH MELBOURNE
TORONTO JOHANNESBURG
AUCKLAND SINGAPORE
IBADAN HONG KONG
NAIROBI

SBN 435 14480 4

Published by Heinemann Educational Books Ltd
48 Charles Street, London W1X 8AH
Printed in Great Britain by Cox & Wyman Ltd
London, Fakenham and Reading

Acknowledgements

The Editor and Publisher wish to thank the following for permission to reprint copyright material: Ted Hughes and Faber & Faber Ltd for 'My Brother Bert' from *Meet my Folks;* Robert Sward and Putnam & Co Ltd for 'Uncle Dog: The Poet at 9' from *Uncle Dog;* Stevie Smith and Longmans Green & Co for 'Nodding', and 'Parrot' from *The Frog Prince;* Denise Levertov, New Directions Publishing Corps Inc and Jonathan Cape Ltd for 'The Rainwalkers' from *The Jacob's Ladder;* Cobden Sanderson for 'Milk for the Cat' and 'God of Dogs' by Harold Monro from *Collected Poems;* Miss D. E. Collins and Methuen & Co Ltd for 'The Song of Quoodle' from *The Flying Inn;* Faber & Faber Ltd for 'Dogs in the Park', 'Jigsaw III', and 'Pet Shop' by Louis MacNeice from *Collected Poems;* Philip Larkin and Faber & Faber Ltd for 'Take One Home for the Kiddies'; Laurence Pollinger Ltd, the Estate of the late Mrs Frieda Lawrence and William Heinemann Ltd for 'Puss Puss!', 'Mountain Lion', 'Bat', 'The Mosquito Knows', 'Self Pity', and 'Elephants in the Circus' from *The Completed Poems of D. H. Lawrence;* Vernon Scannell and Eyre & Spottiswoode Ltd for 'A Case of Murder' from *Walking Wounded;* Mrs Myfanwy Thomas and Faber & Faber Ltd for 'A Cat' from *Collected Poems;* J. M. Dent & Sons for 'The Cat and the Bird' by George Canning from *The Cherry Tree;* Rupert Hart-Davis Ltd and Phoebe Hesketh for 'Cats' in *Prayer for Sun;* James Kirkup and Oxford University Press for 'The Bird Fancier' from *Refusal to Conform;* Mrs H. M. Davies and Jonathan Cape Ltd for 'The Rat' and 'The Rabbit' from *The Complete Poems of W. H. Davies;* Ted Hughes and Faber & Faber Ltd for 'Hawk Roosting' from *Lupercal,* for 'The Jaguar' from *The Hawk in the Rain* and for 'A Moon Man-Hunt' from *The Earth-Owl and Other Moon People;* Eyre & Spottiswoode Ltd for 'The Bird of Night' by Randall Jarrell from *The Lost World;* Faber & Faber Ltd for 'The Pike' and 'Slug' by Theodore Roethke from *Collected Poems;* Adrian Mitchell and Jonathan Cape Ltd for 'The Fox' from *Poems;* Clifford Dyment and J. M. Dent & Sons Ltd for 'Man and Beast' from *Poems 1935–1948;* John Montague and MacGibbon & Kee Ltd for 'The Trout' from *A Chosen Light;* Michael Hamburger and Longmans Green & Co Ltd for 'Old Poacher' from *Weather and Season;* Mr Harold Owen and Chatto & Windus Ltd for 'Arms and the Boy' and 'The Show' from *The Collected Poems of Wilfred Owen;* W. H. Auden and Faber & Faber Ltd for 'O What is That Sound' from *Collected Shorter Poems 1927–1957;* Andrew

vi

Pets

Predators

Pets

My Brother Bert

Ted Hughes

Pets are the Hobby of my brother Bert.
He used to go to school with a Mouse in his shirt.

His Hobby it grew, as some hobbies will,
And grew and grew and GREW until —

Oh don't breathe a word, pretend you haven't heard.
A simply appalling thing has occurred —

The very thought makes me iller and iller:
Bert's brought home a gigantic Gorilla!

If you think that's really not such a scare,
What if it quarrels with his Grizzly Bear?

You still think you could keep your head?
What if the Lion from under the bed

And the four Ostriches that deposit
Their football eggs in his bedroom closet

And the Aardvark out of his bottom drawer
All danced out and joined in the Roar?

What if the Pangolins were to caper
Out of their nests behind the wallpaper?

With the fifty sorts of Bats
That hang on his hatstand like old hats,

And out of a shoebox the excitable Platypus
Along with the Ocelot or Jungle-Cattypus?

The Wombat, the Dingo, the Gecko, the Grampus —
How they would shake the house with their Rumpus!

Not to forget the Bandicoot
Who would certainly peer from his battered old boot.

Why it could be a dreadful day,
And what Oh what would the neighbours say!

3

Uncle Dog: The Poet at 9

Robert Sward

I did not want to be old Mr
Garbage man, but uncle dog
Who rode sitting beside him.

Uncle dog had always looked
To me to be truck-strong
Wise-eyed, a cur-like Ford

Of a dog. I did not want
To be Mr Garbage man because
All he had was cans to do.

Uncle dog sat there me-beside-him
Emptying nothing. Barely even
Looking from garbage side to side:

Like rich people in the backseats
Of chauffeur-cars, only shaggy
In an unwagging tall-scrawny way.

Uncle dog belonged any just where
He sat, but old Mr Garbage man
Had to stop at everysingle can.

I thought. I did not want to be Mr.
Everybody calls them that first.
A dog is said, Dog! Or by name.

I would rather be called Rover
Than Mr. And sit like a tough
Smart mongrel beside a garbage man.

Uncle dog always went to places
Unconcerned, without no hurry.
Independent like some leashless

Toot. Honourable among scavenger
Can-picking dogs. And with a bitch
At every other can. And meat:

His for the barking. Oh, I wanted
To be uncle dog — sharp, high fox-
Eared, cur-Ford truck-faced

4

With his pick of the bones.
A doing, truckman's dog
And not a simple child-dog

Nor friend to man, but an uncle
Travelling, and to himself —
And a bitch at every second can.

Nodding

Stevie Smith

Tizdal my beautiful cat
Lies on the old rag mat
In front of the kitchen fire.
Outside the night is black.

The great fat cat
Lies with his paws under him
His whiskers twitch in a dream,
He is slumbering.

The clock on the mantelpiece
Ticks unevenly, tic-toc, tic-toc,
Good heavens what is the matter
With the kitchen clock?

Outside an owl hunts,
Hee hee hee hee,
Hunting in the Old Park
From his snowy tree.
What on earth can he find in the park tonight,
It is so wintry?

Now the fire burns suddenly too hot
Tizdal gets up to move,
Why should such an animal
Provoke our love?

The twigs from the elder bush
Are tapping on the window pane
As the wind sets them tapping,
Now the tapping begins again.

One laughs on a night like this
In a room half firelight half dark
With a great lump of a cat
Moving on the hearth,
And the twigs tapping quick,
And the owl in an absolute fit.
One laughs supposing creation
Pays for its long plodding
Simply by coming to this –
Cat, night, fire – and a girl nodding.

Me and my Dog

Anon

Me and my dog
   have tramped together
    in cold weather
     and hot.

Me and my dog
   don't care whether
    we get any work
     or not.

The Rainwalkers

Denise Levertov

An old man whose black face
shines golden-brown as wet pebbles
under the streetlamp, is walking
two mongrel dogs of dis-
proportionate size, in the rain,
in the relaxed early-evening avenue.

The small sleek one wants to stop,
docile to the imploring soul of the trashbasket,
but the young tall curly one
wants to walk on; the glistening sidewalk
entices him to arcane happenings.

Increasing rain. The old bareheaded man
smiles and grumbles to himself.
The lights change: the avenue's
endless nave echoes notes of
liturgical red. He drifts

between his dogs' desires.
The three of them are enveloped –
turning now to go crosstown – in their
sense of each other, of pleasure,
of weather, of corners,
of leisurely tensions between them
and private silence.

A Gigantic Beauty of a Stallion

Walt Whitman

A gigantic beauty of a stallion, fresh and responsive to
    my caresses.
Head high in the forehead, wide between the ears,
Limbs glossy and supple, tail dusting the ground,
Eyes full of sparkling wickedness, ears finely cut,
    flexibly moving.
His nostrils dilate as my heels embrace him,
His well-built limbs tremble with pleasure as we race
    around and return.

Private Wealth

Robert Herrick

Though clock
To tell how night draws hence, I've none,
A cock
I have, to sing how day draws on . . .

A hen
I keep, which creeking day by day,
Tells when
She goes her long white egg to lay.

A goose
I have, which, with a jealous ear,
Lets loose
Her tongue, to tell what danger's near.

A lamb
I keep (tame) with my morsels fed,
Whose dam
An orphan left him (lately dead).

A cat
I keep, that plays about my house,
Grown fat,
With eating many a miching mouse.   skulking

To these
A Trasy I do keep, whereby   Herrick's dog
I please
The more my rural privacie:

Which are
But toys, to give my heart some ease:
Where care
None is, slight things do lightly please.

Milk for the Cat

Harold Monro

When the tea is brought at five o'clock,
And all the neat curtains are drawn with care,
The little black cat with bright green eyes
Is suddenly purring there.

At first she pretends, having nothing to do,
She has come in merely to blink by the grate,
But, though tea may be late or the milk may be sour,
She is never late.

And presently her agate eyes
Take a soft large milky haze,
And her independent casual glance
Becomes a stiff hard gaze.

Then she stamps her claws or lifts her ears
Or twists her tail and begins to stir,
Till suddenly all her lithe body becomes
One breathing trembling purr.

The children eat and wriggle and laugh;
The two old ladies stroke their silk:
But the cat is grown small and thin with desire,
Transformed to a creeping lust for milk.

The white saucer like some full moon descends
At last from the clouds of the table above;
She sighs and dreams and thrills and glows,
Transfigured with love.

She nestles over the shining rim,
Buries her chin in the creamy sea;
Her tail hangs loose; each drowsy paw
Is doubled under each bending knee.

A long dim ecstasy holds her life;
Her world is an infinite shapeless white,
Till her tongue has curled the last holy drop,
Then she sinks back into the night,

Draws and dips her body to heap
Her sleepy nerves in the great arm-chair,
Lies defeated and buried deep
Three or four hours unconscious there.

God of Dogs

Harold Monro

Clearly the news has reached us from the skies
Man has no faithful Master always wise,
But dogs are different — Not a dog but can
Believe in one dear God and Master-Man,
Dog has a leash and automatic food
And clear decision for eventual good.
He prays and he is answered. When his creed
Fails him he makes another to his need.
A fortunate reserve of heavenly power
Provides him with a use for every hour.

O, happy dog he cares not to foresee
Eventualities of eternity.
His movements dream through plain existent Now;
No speculations crease his hairy brow,
In his great white religion he can hide
His soul, in its perfectitude abide.
Kick is so swiftly followed by caress,
Sorrow so soon forgotten in blessedness.
He is not tempted ever that he swerve
From the first purpose patiently to serve.
Ask! – He can love. Look! – but he cannot kneel.
Wonder at him! – Oh, what can Dog not feel!
Think if your confident mind of deity can
Of what he must have left, to come to Man.

The swift desirousness of chase by scent
The early ways his natural instinct went –
Watch him discovered in his ancient mood
Brought back to kennel from some park or wood.
See the wild glint in his repentant eyes,
His yap which broke across the grass in cries
Is turned now almost to uncanny tears.
And yet he loves far better than he fears.
His wide eyes change their colour. All his nerves
Move to your hand. His sense not ever swerves
Out of belief. He, patient, loving, true,
Whatever God may purpose or may do,
Follows and will obey. . . .
                                        O, happy beast
Try not to become too wise,
Restrain yourself from mysteries;
Revere your God, respect his laws,
You must not hope to know their cause.
Dog, be a dog contentedly!
Dog, always be my dog to me.
I want no human friend but do
Not ever make me forfeit you.

The Song of Quoodle

G. K. Chesterton

They haven't got no noses,
The fallen sons of Eve;
Even the smell of roses
Is not what they supposes;
But more than mind discloses
And more than men believe.

The brilliant smell of water,
The brave smell of a stone,
The smell of dew and thunder,
The old bones buried under,
Are things in which they blunder
And err, if left alone.

The wind from winter forests,
The scent of scentless flowers,
The breath of brides' adorning,
The smell of snare and warning,
The smell of Sunday morning,
God gave to us for ours.

And Quoodle here discloses
All things that Quoodle can,
They haven't got no noses,
They haven't got no noses,
And goodness only knowses
The Noselessness of Man.

Dogs in the Park

Louis MacNeice

The precise yet furtive etiquette of dogs
Makes them ignore the whistle while they talk
In circles round each other, one-man bonds
Deferred in pauses of this man-made walk
To open vistas to a past of packs

That raven round the stuccoed terraces
And scavenge at the mouth of Stone Age caves;
What man proposes dog on his day disposes
In litter round both human and canine graves,
Then lifts his leg to wash the gravestones clean,

While simultaneously his eyes express
Apology and contempt; his master calls
And at the last and sidelong he returns,
Part heretic, part hack, and jumps and crawls
And fumbles to communicate and fails.

And then they leave the park, the leads are snapped
On to the spiky collars, the tails wag
For no known reason and the ears are pricked
To search through legendary copse and crag
For legendary creatures doomed to die
Even as they, the dogs, were doomed to live.

The Parrot

Thomas Campbell

The following incident, so strongly illustrating the power of
memory and association in the lower animals, is not a fiction. I
heard it many years ago in the Island of Mull, from the family to
whom the bird belonged. – *Author's note.*

The deep affections of the breast
    That Heaven to living things imparts
Are not exclusively possess'd
    By human hearts.

A parrot from the Spanish Main,
    Full young and early caged, came o'er
With bright wings to the black domain
    Of Mulla's shore.

To spicy groves where he had won
    His plumage of resplendent hue,
His native fruits and skies and sun,
    He bade adieu.

For these he changed the smoke of turf,
    A heathery land and misty sky,
And turn'd on rocks and raging surf
    His golden eye.

But petted, in our climate cold
    He lived and chatter'd many a day;
Until with age from green and gold
    His wings grew grey.

At last, when blind and seeming dumb,
    He scolded, laughed, and spoke no more,
A Spanish stranger chanced to come
    To Mulla's shore;

He hailed the bird in Spanish speech;
    The bird in Spanish speech replied,
Flapped round his cage with joyous screech,
    Dropt down, and died.

Parrot

Stevie Smith

The old sick parrot
High in a dingy cage
Sick with malevolent rage
Beadily glutted his furious eye
On the old dark
Chimneys of Noel Park

Far from his jungle green
Over the seas he came
To the yellow skies, to the dripping rain,
To the night of his despair.
And the pavements of his street
Are shining beneath the lamp
With a beauty that's not for one
Born under a tropic sun.

He has croup. His feathered chest
Knows no minute of rest.
High on his perch he sits
And coughs and spits,
Waiting for death to come.
Pray heaven it won't be long.

Pet Shop

Louis MacNeice

Cold blood or warm, crawling or fluttering
Bric-à-brac, all are here to be bought,
Noisy or silent, python or myna,
Fish with long silk trains like dowagers,
Monkeys lost to thought.

In a small tank tiny enamelled
Green terrapin jostle, in a cage a crowd
Of small birds elbow each other and bicker
While beyond the ferrets, eardrum, eyeball
Find that macaw too loud.

Here behind glass lies a miniature desert,
The sand littered with rumpled gauze
Discarded by snakes like used bandages;
In the next door desert fossilized lizards
Stand in a pose, a pause.

But most of the customers want something comfy –
Rabbit, hamster, potto, puss –
Something to hold on the lap and cuddle
Making believe it will return affection
Like some neutered succubus.

Purr then or chirp, you are here for our pleasure,
Here at the mercy of our whim and purse;
Once there was the wild, now tanks and cages,
But we can offer you a home, a haven,
That might prove even worse.

Take One Home for the Kiddies

Philip Larkin

On shallow straw, in shadeless glass,
Huddled by empty bowls, they sleep:
No dark, no dam, no earth, no grass –
Mam, get us one of them to keep.

Living toys are something novel,
But it soon wears off somehow.
Fetch the shoebox, fetch the shovel –
Mam, we're playing funerals now.

Puss-Puss!

D. H. Lawrence

– Oh, Auntie, isn't he a beauty! And is he a gentleman or a lady?
– Neither, my dear! I had him fixed. It saves him from so many
  undesirable associations.

A Case of Murder

Vernon Scannell

They should not have left him there alone,
Alone that is except for the cat.
He was only nine, not old enough
To be left alone in a basement flat,
Alone, that is, except for the cat.
A dog would have been a different thing,
A big gruff dog with slashing jaws,
But a cat with round eyes mad as gold,
Plump as a cushion with tucked-in paws –
Better have left him with a fair-sized rat!
But what they did was leave him with a cat.
He hated that cat; he watched it sit,
A buzzing machine of soft black stuff,
He sat and watched and he hated it,
Snug in its fur, hot blood in a muff,
And its mad gold stare and the way it sat
Crooning dark warmth: he loathed all that.
So he took Daddy's stick and he hit the cat.
Then quick as a sudden crack in glass
It hissed, black flash, to a hiding place
In the dust and dark beneath the couch,
And he followed the grin on his new-made face,
A wide-eyed, frightened snarl of a grin,
And he took the stick and he thrust it in,
Hard and quick in the furry dark.

The black fur squealed and he felt his skin
Prickle with sparks of dry delight.
Then the cat again came into sight,
Shot for the door that wasn't quite shut,
But the boy, quick too, slammed fast the door:
The cat, half-through, was cracked like a nut
And the soft black thud was dumped on the floor.
Then the boy was suddenly terrified
And he bit his knuckles and cried and cried;
But he had to do something with the dead thing there.
His eyes squeezed beads of salty prayer
But the wound of fear gaped wide and raw;
He dared not touch the thing with his hands
So he fetched a spade and shovelled it
And dumped the load of heavy fur
In the spidery cupboard under the stair
Where it's been for years, and though it died
It's grown in that cupboard and its hot low purr
Grows slowly louder year by year:
There'll not be a corner for the boy to hide
When the cupboard swells and all sides split
And the huge black cat pads out of it.

A Cat

Edward Thomas

She had a name among the children;
But no one loved though someone owned
Her, locked her out of doors at bedtime
And had her kittens duly drowned.

In Spring, nevertheless, this cat
Ate blackbirds, thrushes, nightingales,
And birds of bright voice and plume and flight,
As well as scraps from neighbours' pails.

I loathed and hated her for this;
One speckle on a thrush's breast
Was worth a million such; and yet
She lived long, till God gave her rest.

The Cat and the Bird

George Canning

Tell me, tell me, gentle Robin,
What is it sets thy heart a-throbbing?
Is it that Grimalkin fell
Hath killed thy father or thy mother,
Thy sister or thy brother,
Or any other?
Tell me but that,
And I'll kill the Cat.

But stay, little Robin, did you ever spare
A grub on the ground or a fly in the air?
No, that you never did, I'll swear;
So I won't kill the Cat,
That's flat.

The Cat

Mervyn Griffiths (aged 14)

His black feline shape picks itself
Stealthily through the garden to
The bird-table.
He crouches, set to pounce.
And with one gravity-defying leap
He has his prey.

After leaving only feathers and feet
Of his victim,
He trots smugly home, to be
Tame again.

Cats

Phoebe Hesketh

Cats are contradictions; tooth and claw
Velvet-padded;
Snowflake-gentle paw
A fist of pins;
Kettles on the purr
Ready to spit;
Black silk then bristled fur.

Cats are of the East —
Scimitar and sphinx;
Sunlight striped with shade.
Leopard, lion, lynx
Moss-footed in a frightened glade;
Slit-eyes an amber glint
Or boring through the darkness, cool as jade.

Cats have come to rest
Upon the cushioned West.
Here, dyed-in-the-silk,
They lap up bottled milk —
Not that of human kindness —
And return
To the mottled woods of Spring
Making the trees afraid
With leaf and wing
A-flutter at the movement in the fern.

Midnight-wild
With phosphorescent eyes,
Cats are morning-wise
Sleeping as they stare into the sun,
Blind to the light,
Deaf to echoing cries
From a ravaged wood.
Cats see black and white
Morning and night as one.

Predators

Photograph by Lennant Osterlund. By courtesy of the Camera Press.

The Bird-Fancier

James Kirkup

Up to his shoulders
In grasses coarse as silk,
The white cat with the yellow eyes
Sits with all four paws together,
Tall as a quart of milk.

He hardly moves his head
To touch with nice nose
What his wary whiskers tell him
Is here a weed
And here a rose.

On a dry stick he rubs his jaws,
And the thin
Corners of his smile
Silently mew when a leaf
Tickles his chin.

With a neat grimace
He nips a new
Blade of feathery grass,
Flicks from his ear
A grain of dew

His sleepy eyes are wild with birds.
Every sparrow, thrush and wren
Widens their furred horizons
Till their flying song
Narrows them again.

The Tyger

William Blake

Tyger! Tyger! burning bright
In the forests of the night,
What immortal hand or eye
Could frame thy fearful symmetry?

In what distant deeps or skies
Burnt the fire of thine eyes?
On what wings dare he aspire?
What the hand dare seize the fire?

And what shoulder, & what art,
Could twist the sinews of thy heart?
And when thy heart began to beat,
What dread hand? & what dread feet?

What the hammer? what the chain?
In what furnace was thy brain?
What the anvil? what dread grasp
Dare its deadly terrors clasp?

When the stars threw down their spears,
And water'd heaven with their tears,
Did he smile his work to see?
Did he who made the Lamb make thee?

Tyger! Tyger! burning bright
In the forests of the night,
What immortal hand or eye
Dare frame thy fearful symmetry?

The Two Ravens

Anon

There were two ravens who sat on a tree,
and they were black as they could be;
and one of them I heard him say,
Oh where shall we go to dine today?
Shall we go down to the salt, salt sea,
or shall we dine by the greenwood tree?

As I walked down on the white sea sand
I saw a fair ship sailing near at hand.
I waved my wings, I bent my beak,
that ship she sank and I heard a shriek.
There lie the sailors, one, two, and three,
Oh shall we go dine by the wild salt sea?

Come, I shall show you a far better sight –
a lonesome glen, and a new-slain knight:
his blood yet on the grass is hot,
his sword half-drawn, his shafts unshot.
And no one knows that he lies there
but his hound, his hawk, and his lady fair.

His hound is to the hunting gone,
his hawk to fetch the wild fowl home,
his lady's gone to another mate. –
Oh shall we make our feasting sweet!
Our dinner is sure, our feasting is free.
Oh come and we'll dine by the greenwood tree!

Oh you shall tear at his naked white thighs,
and I'll peck out his fair blue eyes.
You can pull a lock of his fine yellow hair
to thicken your nest where it grows bare.
The golden down on his young chin
will do to rest my young ones in.

Oh cold and bare will his bed be
when grey winter storms sing in the tree.
His head's on the turf, at his feet a stone. –
He'll sleep nor hear young maiden's mourn.
Over his white bones the birds will fly,
the wild deer run, the foxes cry.

The Rat

W. H. Davies

'That woman there is almost dead,
Her feet and hands like heavy lead;
Her cat's gone out for his delight,
He will not come again this night.

'Her husband in a pothouse drinks,
Her daughter at a soldier winks;
Her son is at his sweetest game,
Teasing the cobbler old and lame.

'Now with these teeth that powder stones,
I'll pick at one of her cheek-bones:
When husband, son and daughter come,
They'll soon see who was left at home.'

The Hawk

Richard Church

The hawk! He stands on air,
 Treads it down, height over height.
He fixes with his dreadful stare
 One earthbound, furry mite.

Solitary in the sky
 He leans on either wing,
And closes with that cruel eye
 Ten acres in a ring.

Above that sunken realm he rides
 And swoops whene'er he will
On leveret, mouse, and all besides,
 Far chosen for his kill.

The lesser birds unite in fear
 And flutter to attack.
He veers aside as they draw near,
 Hangs poised, and then swerves back.

Alone once more, with pinions spread
 He now resumes his stare
For prey already doomed and dead,
 Though it is unaware.

Fate with talons, fate with wings,
 Fate with unerring eye,
Shadowing all terrestrial things –
 The pinpoint in the sky!

Hawk Roosting

Ted Hughes

I sit in the top of the wood, my eyes closed.
Inaction, no falsifying dream
Between my hooked head and hooked feet:
Or in sleep rehearse perfect kills and eat.

The convenience of the high trees!
The air's buoyancy and the sun's ray
Are of advantage to me;
And the earth's face upward for my inspection.

24

My feet are locked upon the rough bark.
It took the whole of Creation
To produce my foot, my each feather:
Now I hold Creation in my foot

Or fly up, and revolve it all slowly –
I kill where I please because it is all mine.
There is no sophistry in my body: *fulseness (false arguments)*
My manners are tearing off heads – *direct methods.*

The allotment of death.
For the one path of my flight is direct
Through the bones of the living.
No arguments assert my right:

The sun is behind me.
Nothing has changed since I began.
My eye has permitted no change.
I am going to keep things like this.

The Eagle

Lord Tennyson

He clasps the crag with hooked hands; ✳
Close to the sun in lonely lands,
Ring'd with the azure world, he stands.

The wrinkled sea beneath him crawls;
He watches from his mountain walls,
And like a thunderbolt he falls.

The Bird of Night

Randall Jarrell

A shadow is floating through the moonlight.
Its wings don't make a sound.
Its claws are long, its beak is bright.
Its eyes try all the corners of the night.

c

It calls and calls: all the air swells and heaves
And washes up and down like water.
The ear that listens to the owl believes
In death. The bat beneath the eaves,

The mouse beside the stone are still as death.
The owl's air washes them like water.
The owl goes back and forth inside the night,
And the night holds its breath.

Pike

Theodore Roethke

The river turns,
Leaving a place for the eye to rest,
A furred, a rocky pool,
A bottom of water.

The crabs tilt and eat, leisurely,
And the small fish lie, without shadow, motionless,
Or drift lazily in and out of the weeds.
The bottom-stones shimmer back their irregular striations,
And the half-sunken branch bends away from the gazer's eye.

A scene for the self to abjure! —
And I lean, almost into the water,
My eye always beyond the surface reflection;
I lean, and love these manifold shapes,
Until, out from a dark cove,
From beyond the end of a mossy log,
With one sinuous ripple, then a rush,
A thrashing-up of the whole pool,
The pike strikes.

The Fox

Adrian Mitchell

A fox among the shadows of the town,
Should I surrender to the arms of man?

On the blank icehills lies in wait
The fighting cold who has thrown down
His challenge. I'll not imitate
The feline compromise. I scan
With warring eyes the servile fate
Of animals who joined the heated town.

Lean-hearted lions in the concrete zoo
Grow bellies, tendons slacken in pale hide,
  Their breath slows to a dying pace.
  Their keepers love them? Tell me who
  Would cage his love in such a place,
  Where only fish are satisfied?
  The keeper has a huntsman's face,
His grasping love would kill me in the zoo.

A scavenger throughout the snowing wind
I peel the sweet bark from the frozen tree
  Or trap the bird with springing jaws.
  The sun retreats out of my mind.
  How could I give this waking pause
  When death's my sleeping company?
  Mad empty, licking at my sores,
I howl this bitter and unloving wind.

Furious in this savage winter day
The crimson riders hounded me from birth
  Through landscapes built of thorn and stone.
  Though I must be their sudden prey,
  Torn to my terror's skeleton,
  Or go to the forgotten earth;
  I will have hunted, too, alone,
I will have wandered in my handsome day.

Four seasons wrestle me, I throw them all
And live to tumble with another year
  In love or battle. I'll not fly
  From mindless elements and fall
  A victim to the keeper's lie.
  The field is mine; but still I fear
  Strong death, my watching enemy,
Though seasons pass and I survive them all.

Malefactors

Edmund Blunden

Nailed to these green laths long ago,
You cramp and shrivel into dross,
Blotched with mildews, gnawed with moss,
And now the eye can scarcely know
The snake among you from the kite,
    So sharp does Death's fang bite.

I guess your stories; you were shot
Hovering above the miller's chicks;
And you, coiled on his threshold bricks –
Hissing you died; and you, sir Stoat,
Dazzled with stablemen's lantern stood
    And tasted crabtree wood.

Here then you leered-at luckless churls,
Clutched to your clumsy gibbet, shrink
To shapeless orts; hard by the brink
Of this black scowling pond that swirls
To turn the wheel beneath the mill,
    The wheel so long since still.

There's your revenge, the wheel at tether,
The miller gone, the white planks rotten,
The very name of the mill forgotten,
Dimness and silence met together.
Felons of fur and feather, can
    There lurk some crime in man,

In man your executioner,
Whom here Fate's cudgel battered down?
Did he too filch from squire and clown?
The damp gust makes the ivy whirr
Like passing death; the sluices well,
    Dreary as a passing-bell.

Man and Beast

Clifford Dyment

Hugging the ground by the lilac tree,
With shadows in conspiracy,

The black cat from the house next door
Waits with death in each bared claw

For the tender unwary bird
That all the summer I have heard

In the orchard singing. I hate
The cat that is its savage fate,

And choose a stone with which to send
Slayer, not victim, to its end.

I look to where the black cat lies,
But drop my stone, seeing its eyes —

Who is it sins now, those eyes say,
You the hunter, or I the prey?

The Trout

John Montague

Flat on the bank I parted
Rushes to ease my hands
In the water without a ripple
And tilt them slowly downstream
To where he lay, light as a leaf,
In his fluid sensual dream.

Bodiless lord of creation
I hung briefly above him
Savouring my own absence
Senses expanding in the slow
Motion, the photographic calm
That grows before action.

As the curve of my hands
Swung under his body
He surged, with visible pleasure.
I was so preternaturally close
I could count every stipple
But still cast no shadow, until

The two palms crossed in a cage
Under the lightly pulsing gills.
Then (entering my own enlarged
Shape, which rode on the water)
I gripped. To this day I can
Taste his terror on my hands.

Old Poacher

Michael Hamburger

Learned in woods
As troubador in words,
Delicate as a troubador's lady,
Killer of does grown doe-like
In nostril, ear,
Lithely, gravely he stalks
His quarry
That will never know death.
And men stalk him.

Only a hawk cries
Above the clearing;
Robin and blackbird are still.
It is the hawk will cry
Till his eye meets
The man's eye
And silent he dips over oak-tops
In flight that is not fear
But hunger's cunning.

Fearless, wily, the man
Listens:
For dog's pad on moss, dry leaves,
Brushed fern, torn bramble,
Panting breath, cough,
Squelch of boot in trough;
Or cropped grass,
Nibble on low hazel bough,
Scuttle of hoof, claw.

And feels again
The thorny joy
Of his great indifference:

To have almost forgotten death
In the woods, in hunger's
Mastery over fear;
With senses grown
Reliable, reliant,
And a man's mind
To savour the sense —
Hunting, hunted, both hawk and deer.

Arms and the Boy

Wilfred Owen

Let the boy try along this bayonet-blade
How cold steel is, and keen with hunger of blood;
Blue with all malice, like a madman's flash;
And thinly drawn with famishing for flesh.

Lend him to stroke these blind, blunt bullet-leads
Which long to nuzzle in the hearts of lads,
Or give him cartridges of fine zinc teeth,
Sharp with the sharpness of grief and death.

For his teeth seem for laughing round an apple.
There lurk no claws behind his fingers supple;
And God will grow no talons at his heels,
Nor antlers through the thickness of his curls.

The Slave in the Dismal Swamp

H. W. Longfellow

In dark fens of the Dismal Swamp
   The hunted Negro lay;
He saw the fire of the midnight camp,
And heard at times a horse's tramp
   And a bloodhound's distant bay.

Where will-o'-the-wisps and glow-worms shine,
   In bulrush and in brake;
Where waving mosses shroud the pine,
And cedar grows, and the poisonous vine
   Is spotted like the snake;

Where hardly a human foot could pass,
  Or a human heart would dare,
On the quaking turf of the green morass
He crouched in the rank and tangled grass,
  Like a wild beast in his lair.

A poor old slave, infirm and lame;
  Great scars deformed his face;
On his forehead he bore the brand of shame,
And the rags, that hid his mangled frame,
  Were the livery of disgrace.

All things above were bright and fair,
  All things were glad and free;
Lithe squirrels darted here and there,
And wild birds filled the echoing air
  With songs of Liberty!

On him alone was the doom of pain,
  From the morning of his birth;
On him alone the curse of Cain
Fell, like a flail on the garnered grain,
  And struck him to the earth!

O What is That Sound

W. H. Auden

O what is that sound which so thrills the ear
  Down in the valley drumming, drumming?
Only the scarlet soldiers, dear,
  The soldiers coming.

O what is that light I see flashing so clear
  Over the distance brightly, brightly?
Only the sun on their weapons, dear,
  As they step lightly.

O what are they doing with all that gear,
  What are they doing this morning, this morning?
Only their usual manoeuvres, dear,
  Or perhaps a warning.

O why have they left the road down there,
    Why are they suddenly wheeling, wheeling?
Perhaps a change in their orders, dear,
    Why are you kneeling?

O haven't they stopped for the doctor's care,
    Haven't they reined their horses, their horses?
Why, they are none of them wounded, dear,
    None of these forces.

O is it the parson they want, with white hair,
    Is it the parson, is it, is it?
No, they are passing his gateway, dear,
    Without a visit.

O it must be the farmer who lives so near.
    It must be the farmer so cunning, so cunning?
They have passed the farmyard already, dear,
    And now they are running.

O where are you going? Stay with me here!
    Were the vows you swore deceiving, deceiving?
No, I promised to love you, dear,
    But I must be leaving.

O it's broken the lock and splintered the door,
    O it's the gate where they're turning, turning;
Their boots are heavy on the floor
    And their eyes are burning.

Man, the Man-Hunter

Carl Sandburg

I saw Man, the man-hunter,
Hunting with a torch in one hand
And kerosene can in the other,
Hunting with guns, ropes, shackles.

33

I listened
And the high cry rang,
The high cry of Man, the man-hunter:
We'll get you yet, you sbxyzch!

I listened later.
The high cry rang:
Kill him! kill him! the sbxyzch!

In the morning the sun saw
Two butts of something, a smoking rump,
And a warning in charred wood:
Well, we got him,
the sbxyzch.

The Show

Wilfred Owen

We have fallen in the dreams the ever-living
Breathe on the tarnished mirror of the world,
And then smooth out with ivory hands and sigh.
W. B. Yeats

My soul looked down from a vague height, with Death
As unremembering how I rose or why,
And saw a sad land, weak with sweats of dearth,
Gray, cratered like the moon with hollow woe,
And pitted with great pocks and scabs of plagues.

Across its beard, that horror of harsh wire,
There moved thin caterpillars, slowly uncoiled.
It seemed they pushed themselves to be as plugs
Of ditches, where they writhed and shrivelled, killed.

By them had slimy paths been trailed and scraped
Round myriad warts that might be little hills.

From gloom's last dregs these long-strung creatures crept,
And vanished out of dawn down hidden holes.

(And smell came up from those foul openings
As out of mouths, or deep wounds deepening.)

On dithering feet upgathered, more and more,
Brown strings, towards strings of gray, with bristling spines,
All migrants from green fields, intent on mire.

Those that were gray, of more abundant spawns,
Ramped on the rest and ate them and were eaten.

I saw their bitten backs curve, loop, and straighten,
I watched those agonies curl, lift, and flatten.
Whereat, in terror what that sight might mean,
I reeled and shivered earthward like a feather.

And Death fell with me, like a deepening moan.
And He, picking a manner of worm, which half had hid
Its bruises in the earth, but crawled no further,
Showed me its feet, the feet of many men,
And the fresh-severed head of it, my head.

Encounters

Detail of an etching. Photograph by Tom Biro.

Field-Glasses

Andrew Young

Though buds still speak in hints
And frozen ground has set the flints
As fast as precious stones
And birds perch on the boughs, silent as cones,

Suddenly waked from sloth
Young trees put on a ten years' growth
And stones double their size,
Drawn nearer through field-glasses' greater eyes.

Why I borrow their sight
Is not to give birds a fright
Creeping up close by inches;
I make the trees come, bringing tits and finches.

I lift a field itself
As lightly as I might a shelf,
And the rooks do not rage
Caught for a moment in my crystal cage.

And while I stand and look,
Their private lives an open book,
I feel so privileged
My shoulders prick, as though they were half-fledged.

March Hares

Andrew Young

I made myself as a tree,
No withered leaf twirling on me;
No, not a bird that stirred my boughs,
As looking out from wizard brows
I watched those lithe and lovely forms
That raised the leaves in storms.

I watched them leap and run,
Their bodies hollowed in the sun
To thin transparency,
That I could clearly see
The shallow colour of their blood
Joyous in love's full flood.

I was content enough,
Watching that serious game of love,
That happy hunting in the wood
Where the pursuer was the more pursued,
To stand in breathless hush
With no more life myself than tree or bush.

A Bird Came down the Walk

Emily Dickinson

A bird came down the walk:
He did not know I saw;
He bit an angle-worm in halves
And ate the fellow, raw.

And then he drank a dew
From a convenient grass,
And then hopped sidewise to the wall
To let a beetle pass.

He glanced with rapid eyes
That hurried all abroad —
They looked like frightened beads, I thought.
He stirred his velvet head

Like one in danger; cautious,
I offered him a crumb,
And he unrolled his feathers
And rowed him softer home

Than oars divide the ocean,
Too silver for a seam,
Or butterflies, off banks of noon,
Leap, plashless, as they swim.

Pitchfork Department

D. J. Enright

It was patent in this ancient city, paradise of
Statuary, that pigeons lacked respect for greatness.
Lucky statesmen, innocent generals and forgiven thinkers,

Their iron breasts befouled, their noble brows
Turned grey, their swords and croziers rusted,
Manuscripts illuminated, padded shanks gone leprous.

Yet the children loved the pigeons, it pleased the
Taxpayers to be used as perches. They walked our streets,
Sometimes were run over, did not disdain our bread.

So the city fathers, as humane as is befitting
In this age of letters and elections, set out
Drugged fodder: 'Let the sleeping birds be stacked

With care in corporation vehicles, and conveyed to
Some remote and rural district. Let them there be laid
In appropriate positions in their proper places.'

They slept the weekend through, lost in a dream
Of the Hall of the Thirty Thousand Buddhas, or the day
When every civil servant shall be issued with a public statue.

On Tuesday afternoon, from under their umbrellas,
The city fathers watched the homing pigeons, assiduous,
    unresenting.
Bowels gently stimulated, natural functions unaffected.

Myxomatosis

Philip Larkin

Caught in the centre of a soundless field
While hot inexplicable hours go by
What trap is this? Where were its teeth concealed?
You seem to ask.
              I make a sharp reply,
Then clean my stick. I'm glad I can't explain
Just in what jaws you were to suppurate:
You may have thought things would come right again
If you could only keep quite still and wait.

Slug

Theodore Roethke

How I loved one like you when I was little! –
With his stripes of silver and his small house on his back,
Making a slow journey around the well-curb.
I longed to be like him, and was,
In my way, close cousin
To the dirt, my knees scrubbing
The gravel, my nose wetter than his.

When I slip, just slightly, in the dark,
I know it isn't a wet leaf,
But you, loose toe from the old life,
The cold slime come into being,
A fat, five-inch appendage
Creeping slowly over the wet grass,
Eating the heart out of my garden.

And you refuse to die decently! –
Flying upward through the knives of my lawnmower
Like pieces of smoked eel or raw oyster,
And I go faster in my rage to get done with it,
Until I'm scraping and scratching at you, on the doormat,
The small dead pieces sticking under an instep;
Or, poisoned, dragging a white skein of spittle over a path –
Beautiful, in its way, like quicksilver –
You shrink to something less,
A rain-drenched fly or spider.

I'm sure I've been a toad, one time or another.
With bats, weasels, worms – I rejoice in the kinship.
Even the caterpillar I can love, and the various vermin.
But as for you, most odious –
Would Blake call you holy?

The Killer

Judith Wright

The day was clear as fire,
the birds sang frail as glass,
when thirsty I came to the creek
and fell by its side in the grass.

My breast on the bright moss
and shower-embroidered weeds,
my lips to the live water,
I saw him turn in the reeds.

Black horror sprang from the dark
in a violent birth,
and through its cloth of grass
I felt the clutch of earth.

O beat him into the ground.
O strike him till he dies,
or else your life itself
drains through those colourless eyes.

I struck again and again.
Slender in black and red
he lies, and his icy glance
turns outward, clear and dead.

But nimble my enemy
as water is, or wind.
He has slipped from his death aside
and vanished into my mind.

He has vanished whence he came,
my nimble enemy;
and the ants come out to the snake
and drink at his shallow eye.

Mountain Lion

D. H. Lawrence

Climbing through the January snow, into the Lobo Canyon
Dark grow the spruce-trees, blue is the balsam, water sounds
    still unfrozen, and the trail is still evident.

Men!
Two men!
Men! The only animal in the world to fear!

They hesitate.
We hesitate.
They have a gun.
We have no gun.

Then we all advance, to meet.

Two Mexicans, strangers, emerging out of the dark and snow
    and inwardness of the Lobo valley.
What are they doing here on this vanishing trail?

What is he carrying?
Something yellow.
A deer?

Qué tiene, amigo?
León —

He smiles, foolishly, as if he were caught doing wrong.
And we smile, foolishly, as if we didn't know.
He is quite gentle and dark-faced.

It is a mountain lion,
A long, long slim cat, yellow like a lioness.
Dead.

He trapped her this morning, he says, smiling foolishly.

Lift up her face,
Her round, bright face, bright as frost.
Her round, fine-fashioned head, with two dead ears;
And stripes in the brilliant frost of her face, sharp, fine dark rays,
Dark, keen, fine rays in the brilliant frost of her face.
Beautiful dead eyes.

Hermoso es!

They go out towards the open;
We go on into the gloom of Lobo.
And above the trees I found her lair,
A hole in the blood-orange brilliant rocks that stick up, a little
    cave.
And bones, and twigs, and a perilous ascent.

So, she will never leap up that way again, with the yellow flash
    of a mountain lion's long shoot!
And her bright striped frost-face will never watch any more, out
    of the shadow of the cave in the blood-orange rock,
Above the trees of the Lobo dark valley-mouth!

Instead, I look out.
And out to the dim of the desert, like a dream, never real;
To the snow of the Sangre de Cristo mountains, the ice of the
mountains of Picoris,
And near across at the opposite steep of snow, green trees
motionless standing in snow, like a Christmas toy.

And I think in this empty world there was room for me and a
mountain lion.
And I think in the world beyond, how easily we might spare a
million or two of humans
And never miss them.
Yet what a gap in the world, the missing white frost-face of that
slim yellow mountain lion!

Lobo

Bat

D. H. Lawrence

At evening, sitting on this terrace,
When the sun from the west, beyond Pisa, beyond the mountains
of Carrara
Departs, and the world is taken by surprise . . .

When the tired flower of Florence is in gloom beneath the
glowing
Brown hills surrounding . . .
When under the arches of the Ponte Vecchio
A green light enters against stream, flush from the west,
Against the current of obscure Arno . . .

Look up, and you see things flying
Between the day and the night;
Swallows with spools of dark thread sewing the shadows
together.

A circle swoop, and a quick parabola under the bridge arches
Where light pushes through;
A sudden turning upon itself of a thing in the air.
A dip to the water.

And you think:
'The swallows are flying so late!'

Swallows?

Dark air-life looping
Yet missing the pure loop . . .
A twitch, a twitter, an elastic shudder in flight
And serrated wings against the sky,
Like a glove, a black glove thrown up at the light,
And falling back.

Never swallows!
Bats!
The swallows are gone.

At a wavering instant the swallows give way to bats
By the Ponte Vecchio . . .
Changing guard.

Bats, and an uneasy creeping in one's scalp
As the bats swoop overhead!
Flying madly.

Pipistrello!
Black piper on an infinitesimal pipe.
Little lumps that fly in air and have voices indefinite, wildly
    vindictive;

Wings like bits of umbrella.

Bats!

Creatures that hang themselves up like an old rag, to sleep;
And disgustingly upside down.
Hanging upside down like rows of disgusting old rags
And grinning in their sleep.
Bats!

In China the bat is symbol of happiness.

Not for me!

The Image

Roy Fuller

A spider in the bath. The image noted:
Significant maybe but surely cryptic.
A creature motionless and rather bloated,
The barriers shining, vertical and white:
Passing concern, and pity mixed with spite.

Next day with some surprise one finds it there.
It seems to have moved an inch or two, perhaps.
It starts to take on that familiar air
Of prisoners for whom time is erratic:
The filthy aunt forgotten in the attic.

Quite obviously it came up through the waste,
Rejects through ignorance or apathy
That passage back. The problem must be faced;
And life go on though strange intruders stir
Among its ordinary furniture.

One jibs at murder, so a sheet of paper
Is slipped beneath the accommodating legs.
The bathroom window shows for the escaper
The lighted lanterns of laburnum hung
In copper beeches – on which scene it's flung.

We certainly would like thus easily
To cast out of the house all suffering things.
But sadness and responsibility
For our own kind lives in the image noted:
A half-loved creature, motionless and bloated.

Hunting with a Stick

Michael Baldwin

Once, ten years old, in the cobweb sun
I chased a rabbit on stiffening grass
Till it twinkled into its hole of sand.
Although I knew that the hunt was done
(For rabbits burrow deeper than fire)
I crouched and crept there, stretching my hand,

And kneeling my shadow on frost I saw
In a turn of the hole too tight to pass
Its fluffed fat haunches were firmly jammed,
Its white tail sat as still as a star.

The moment froze in a single breath:
Give me a second and I could be quick,
Having spent ten years in the ways of death,
And I wanted this death, not one planned.
I thrust at its buttocks with my stick
And felt the soft bone go under the fur,
The silence I knelt on echo and stir,
The green meat of mornings that made me sick . . .

I dragged it back by a fistful of hair,
Then flourished my prize with a dripping claw;
But dangling it upwards again I saw
Its face was bitten and muffled in blood,
One eye was empty and showed the skull,
The soft jaw was eaten into a snarl,
Death hung from its ears in a glistening hood.

And at ten years old I first understood
There were other deaths in the world than me,
More ways to kill than with stone and stick:
While my shadow falconed it from the air
A stoat had sat in its horror there
And bitten its burrowing bone to the quick.

Travelling through the Dark

William Stafford

Travelling through the dark I found a deer
dead on the edge of the Wilson River road.
It is usually best to roll them into the canyon:
that road is narrow; to swerve might make more dead.

By glow of the tail-light I stumbled back of the car
and stood by the heap, a doe, a recent killing;
she had stiffened already, almost cold.
I dragged her off; she was large in the belly.

My fingers touching her side brought me the reason —
her side was warm; her fawn lay there waiting,
alive, still, never to be born.
Beside that mountain road I hesitated.

The car aimed ahead its lowered parking lights;
under the hood purred the steady engine.
I stood in the glare of the warm exhaust turning red;
around our group I could hear the wilderness listen.

I thought hard for us all — my only swerving —
then pushed her over the edge into the river.

An Advancement of Learning

Seamus Heaney

I took the embankment path
(As always, deferring
The bridge). The river nosed past,
Pliable, oil-skinned, wearing

A transfer of gables and sky.
Hunched over the railing,
Well away from the road now, I
Considered the dirty-keeled swans.

Something slobbered curtly, close,
Smudging the silence: a rat
Slimed out of the water and
My throat sickened so quickly that

I turned down the path in cold sweat
But God, another was nimbling
Up the far bank, tracing its wet
Arcs on the stones. Incredibly then

I established a dreaded
Bridgehead. I turned to stare
With deliberate, thrilled care
At my hitherto snubbed rodent.

He clockworked aimlessly a while,
Stopped, back bunched and glistening,
Ears plastered down on his knobbed skull,
Insidiously listening.

The tapered tail that followed him,
The raindrop eye, the old snout:
One by one I took all in.
He trained on me. I stared him out

Forgetting how I used to panic
When his grey brothers scraped and fed
Behind the hen-coop in our yard,
On ceiling boards above my bed.

This terror, cold, wet-furred, small-clawed,
Retreated up a pipe of sewage.
I stared a minute after him.
Then I walked on and crossed the bridge.

Death of a Bird in January

Philip Callow

It is on the grit of the road,
A dead starling, looking big,
With a blackish speckled body
And a beak like a long spike.
It is all beak and bony claws.

You exclaim from pity and stoop down,
Taking the bird very tenderly
In your gloved hand,
While our child pushes close.
She wants to feel and examine it,
She would pull it apart
From sheer exuberant curiosity,
Not cruel. You hold her off
And stand murmuring, rooted,
Asking if it is alive,
Grieving and staring down
And wrapping it in warm breath,
Until I have gone on, shouting:
'Let it rest in peace!'

For I think: All this tenderness
Is against nature, so why bother?
I am growing a tough skin
So as to live in this world.
I am a man. Stiff and churlish
I walk on, secretly moved.
You are generous without reason like a sun.

The Squirrel

Iain Crichton Smith

The squirrel lay on the cold stone
seeming at first a rat, so dead and brown
I didn't dare go near it, for the shudder
of cold distaste and a hot primitive fear.

Flattened it lay, splayed on that cold distaste
as if a car had flung it, like the waste
spun from a turning axle. It was then
someone picked it up so limp and brown

and showed us it was squirrel. Thus at ease
because of the clear dryness of the trees
my eyes could study it. Quite still and pale
I twitched along it from the head to tail

but the tail was missing. And I thought with fear.
What death destroyed you? What has bitten there?
Or tugged it clear, whether alive or dead?
A seesaw forest shivered in my head

thinking – a ferret. Or a boy perhaps
in all that darkness, all the sparkling gaps
alive with venomous green. Till I looked down
and touched it, trembling. Empty and quite brown

it did not shiver. Only I remained
with shock on shock biting my shaking mind
and thinking: Dear one, better to be man,
though pain assaults us, from the trees come down.

The Mosquito Knows

D. H. Lawrence

The mosquito knows full well, small as he is
he's a beast of prey.
But after all
he only takes his bellyful,
he doesn't put my blood in the bank.

I Think I Could Turn and Live with Animals

Walt Whitman

I think I could turn and live with animals, they're so placid and
    self-contain'd,
I stand and look at them long and long.

They do not sweat and whine about their condition,
They do not lie awake in the dark and weep for their sins,
They do not make me sick discussing their duty to God,
Not one is dissatisfied, not one is demented with the mania of
    owning things,
Not one kneels to another, nor to his kind that lived thousands
    of years ago,
Not one is respectable or unhappy over the whole earth.

Self-Pity

D. H. Lawrence

I never saw a wild thing
sorry for itself.
A small bird will drop frozen dead from a bough
without ever having felt sorry for itself.

An August Midnight

Thomas Hardy

I

A shaded lamp and a waving blind,
And the beat of a clock from a distant floor:
On this scene enter – winged, horned, and spined –
A longlegs, a moth, and a dumbledore;
While 'mid my page there idly stands
A sleepy fly, that rubs its hands . . .

II

Thus meet we five, in this still place,
At this point of time, at this point in space.
– My guests besmear my new-penned line,
Or bang at the lamp and fall supine.
'God's humblest, they!' I muse. Yet why?
They know Earth-secrets that know not I.

Birds

Judith Wright

Whatever the bird is, is perfect in the bird.
Weapon kestrel hard as a blade's curve,
thrush round as a mother or a full drop of water,
fruit-green parrot wise in his shrieking swerve –
all are what bird is and do not reach beyond bird.

Whatever the bird does is right for the bird to do –
cruel kestrel dividing in his hunger the sky,
thrush in the trembling dew beginning to sing,
parrot clinging and quarrelling and veiling his queer eye –
all these are as birds are and good for birds to do.

But I am torn and beleaguered by my own people.
The blood that feeds my heart is the blood they gave me,
and my heart is the house where they gather and fight for
    dominion –
all different, all with a wish and a will to save me,
to turn me into the ways of other people.

If I could leave their battleground for the forest of a bird
I could melt the past, the present and the future in one
and find the words that lie behind all these languages.
Then I could fuse my passions into one clear stone
and be simple to myself as the bird is to the bird.

Jigsaw III

Louis MacNeice

The gulf between us and the brutes,
Though deep, seems not too wide. Their games,
Though played with neither bats nor boots,
Though played with neither rules nor names,
Seem motivated much as ours —
Not mentioning hungers lusts and fears.

Cow flicking tail, cat sharpening claws,
Dolphin a-gambol, bird a-wheel —
Transpose our hands to fins, to paws,
To wings, we more or less can feel
The same as they; the intellect
Is all we add to it, or subtract.

The iceberg of our human lives
Being but marginal in air,
Our lonely eminence derives
From the submerged nine-tenths we share
With all the rest who also run,
Shuddering through the shuddering main.

Victims

By courtesy of the Camera Press.

Caring for Animals

Jon Silkin

I ask sometimes why these small animals
With bitter eyes, why we should care for them.

I question the sky, the serene blue water,
But it cannot say. It gives no answer.

And no answer releases in my head
A procession of grey shades patched and whimpering,

Dogs with clipped ears, wheezing cart horses
A fly without shadow and without thought.

Is it with these menaces to our vision
With this procession led by a man carrying wood

We must be concerned? The holy land, the rearing
Green island should be kindlier than this.

Yet the animals, our ghosts, need tending to.
Take in the whipped cat and the blinded owl;

Take up the man-trapped squirrel upon your shoulder.
Attend to the unnecessary beasts.

From growing mercy and a moderate love
Great love for the human animal occurs.

And your love grows. Your great love grows and grows.

The Early Purges

Seamus Heaney

I was six when I first saw kittens drown.
Dan Taggart pitched them, 'the scraggy wee shits',
Into a bucket; a frail metal sound,

Soft paws scraping like mad. But their tiny din
Was soon soused. They were slung on the snout
Of the pump and the water pumped in.

E

'Sure isn't it better for them now?' Dan said.
Like wet gloves they bobbed and shone till he sluiced
Them out on the dunghill, glossy and dead.

Suddenly frightened, for days I sadly hung
Round the yard, watching the three sogged remains
Turn mealy and crisp as old summer dung

Until I forgot them. But the fear came back
When Dan trapped big rats, snared rabbits, shot crows
Or, with a sickening tug, pulled old hens' necks.

Still, living displaces false sentiments
And now, when shrill pups are prodded to drown
I just shrug, 'Bloody pups'. It makes sense:

'Prevention of cruelty' talk cuts ice in town
Where they consider death unnatural,
But on well-run farms pests have to be kept down.

Song of the Battery Hen

Edwin Brock

We can't grumble about accommodation:
we have a new concrete floor that's
always dry, four walls that are
painted white, and a sheet-iron roof
the rain drums on. A fan blows warm air
beneath our feet to disperse the smell
of chicken-shit and, on dull days,
fluorescent lighting sees us.

You can tell me: if you come by
the North door, I am in the twelfth pen
on the left-hand side of the third row
from the floor; and in that pen
I am usually the middle one of three.
But, even without directions, you'd
discover me. I have the same orange-
red comb, yellow beak and auburn
feathers, but as the door opens and you
hear above the electric fan a kind of
one-word wail, I am the one
who sounds loudest in my head.

Listen. Outside this house there's an
orchard with small moss-green apple
trees; beyond that, two fields of
cabbages; then, on the far side of
the road, a broiler house. Listen:
one cockerel grows out of there, as
tall and proud as the first hour of the sun.
Sometimes I stop calling with the others
to listen, and wonder if he hears me.

The next time you come here, look for me.
Notice the way I sound inside my head.
God made us all quite differently,
and blessed us with this expensive home.

Both Harvests

Ken Smith

Guns twitch the gloved ears of the rabbit,
that ripened with the corn. Summer
was burrowed, with the young peering
over green shoots. Now they move
under red corn. But blades are set
and honed. A tractor roves the scythed
edges. These men who stook and bend,
bend and stook, have their business
with grain. Those who come after,
come to kill, gun under shoulder.
A rabbit is a grey thing running,
stopped, hung in air, dead. Some
hide under bound sheaves. Some panic
into the mower and are savaged, blood,
bone, and pelt. Set blades are determined.
Rabbits die running, not like standing grain
cut clean. The field is clear, its straw
lined and ordered: it will be bread
and bedding for safe cattle. The rabbit
need not fear the winter. Shot corpses
brace under fur, are shared out evenly.

The Rabbit

W. H. Davies

Not even when the early birds
Danced on my roof with showery feet
Such music as will come from rain –
Not even then could I forget
The rabbit in his hours of pain;
Where, lying in an iron trap,
He cries all through the deafened night –
Until his smiling murderer comes,
To kill him in the morning light.

Donkey's Dream

Mary Nicholson (aged 13)

Stubborn and stupid
(Or so people say),
Long ears, grey-faced,
Harsh deafening bray.

Coat like grey velvet,
Large sorrowful eyes.
They say, 'Ignorant people,
You heed not my cries.

'You work me and beat me
And don't understand
My dreams of a pleasant
Faraway land,

'Where all of the animals
Live free happy lives,
And for no idle human
Toils and strives.

'But back to this cruel land
I'm brought with a crack
Of my owner's long whip
Striking my back.'

The Mad Yak

Gregory Corso

I am watching them churn the last milk
    they'll ever get from me.
They are waiting for me to die;
They want to make buttons out of my bones.
Where are my sisters and brothers?
That tall monk there, loading my uncle,
    he has a new cap.
And that idiot student of his –
    I never saw that muffler before.
Poor uncle, he lets them load him.
How sad he is, how tired!
I wonder what they'll do with his bones?
And that beautiful tail!
How many shoelaces will they make of that!

Badger

John Clare

When midnight comes a host of dogs and men
Go out and track the badger to his den,
And put a sack within the hole, and lie
Till the old grunting badger passes by.
He comes and hears – they let the strongest loose.
The old fox hears the noise and drops the goose.
The poacher shoots and hurries from the cry,
And the old hare half wounded buzzes by.
They get a forkèd stick to bear him down.
And clap the dogs and take him to the town,
And bait him all the day with many dogs,
And laugh and shout and fright the scampering hogs.
He runs along and bites at all he meets:
They shout and hollo down the noisy streets.

He turns about to face the loud uproar
And drives the rebels to their very door.
The frequent stone is hurled where'er they go;
When badgers fight, then every one's a foe.
The dogs are clapt and urged to join the fray;
The badger turns and drives them all away.
Though scarcely half as big, demure and small,
He fights with dogs for hours and beats them all.

The heavy mastiff, savage in the fray,
Lies down and licks his feet and turns away.
The bulldog knows his match and waxes cold,
The badger grins and never leaves his hold.
He drives the crowd and follows at their heels
And bites them through – the drunkard swears and reels.

The frighted women take the boys away,
The blackguard laughs and hurries on the fray.
He tries to reach the woods, an awkward race,
But sticks and cudgels quickly stop the chase.
He turns agen and drives the noisy crowd
And beats the many dogs in noises loud.
He drives away and beats them every one,
And then they loose them all and set them on.
He falls as dead and kicked by boys and men,
Then starts and grins and drives the crowd agen;
Till kicked and torn and beaten out he lies
And leaves his hold and cackles, groans, and dies.

Beagles

W. R. Rodgers

Over rock and wrinkled ground
Ran the lingering nose of hound,
The little and elastic hare
Stretched herself nor stayed to stare.

Stretched herself, and far away
Darted through the chinks of day,
Behind her, shouting out her name,
The whole blind world galloping came.

Over hills a running line
Curled like a whip-lash, fast and fine,
Past me sailed the sudden pack
Along the taut and tingling track.

From the far flat scene each shout
Like jig-saw piece came tumbling out,
I took and put them all together,
And then they turned into a tether.

A tether that held me to the hare
Here, there, and everywhere.

Reynard the Fox

John Masefield

The fox was strong, he was full of running,
He could run for an hour and then be cunning,
But the cry behind him made him chill,
They were nearer now and they meant to kill.
They meant to run him until his blood
Clogged on his heart as his brush with mud,
Till his back bent up and his tongue hung flagging,
And his belly and brush were filthed with dragging.
Till he crouched stone-still, dead-beat and dirty,
With nothing but teeth against the thirty.
And all the way to that blinding end
He would meet with men and have none his friend:
Men to holloa and men to run him,
With stones to stagger and yells to stun him;
Men to head him, with whips to beat him,
Teeth to mangle, and mouths to eat him.
And all the way, that wild high crying.
To cold his blood with the thought of dying,
The horn and the cheer, and the drum-like thunder
Of the horsehooves stamping the meadows under.
He upped his brush and went with a will
For the Sarsen Stones on Wan Dyke Hill. . . .

For a minute he ran and heard no sound,
Then a whimper came from a questing hound,
Then a 'This way, beauties', and then 'Leu, Leu',
The floating laugh of the horn that blew.
Then the cry again, and the crash and rattle
Of the shrubs burst back as they ran to battle,
Till the woods behind seemed risen from root,
Crying and crashing, to give pursuit,
Till the trees seemed hounds and the air seemed cry,
And the earth so far that he needs must die,
Die where he reeled in the woodland dim,
With a hound's white grips in the spine of him.
For one more burst he could spurt, and then
Wait for the teeth, and the wrench, and men.

He made his spurt for the Mourne End rocks
The air blew rank with the taint of fox;
The yews gave way to a greener space
Of great stone strewn in a grassy place.
And there was his earth at the great grey shoulder
Sunk in the ground, of a granite boulder.
A dry, deep burrow, with rocky roof,
Proof against crowbars, terrier-proof,
Life to the living, rest for bones.

The earth was stopped; it was filled with stones.

A Moon Man-Hunt

Ted Hughes

A man-hunt on the moon is full of horrible sights and sounds.
There are these foxes in red jackets, they are their own horses and
    hounds.
They have unhuman eyes, O they are savage out of all bounds.

They swagger at the meet, their grins going back under their ears.
They are sociable to begin with, showing each other their long
    fangs and their no fears.
They pretend it is all a good game and nothing to do with death
    and its introductory tears.

Now one yip! and they are off, tails waving in sinister accord.
To tell the truth, they are a murderous depraved-looking horde.
Sniff sniff! they come over the acres, till some strolling squire
    looks up and sees them pattering toward.

The sweat jumps on his brow freezingly and the hair stands on
    his thighs.
His lips writhe, his tongue fluffs dry as a duster, tears pour from
    his eyes.
His bowels twist like a strong snake, and for some seconds he
    sways there useless with terrified surprise.

'Ha ha!' go all the foxes in unison.
'That menace, that noble rural vermin, the gentry, there's one!'
The dirt flies from their paws and the squire begins hopelessly to
    run.

But what chance does that wretch have against such an animal?
Five catch his heels, and one on his nose, and ten on each arm,
    he goes down with a yell.
It is terrible, it is terrible, O it is terrible!

The Sportsman

Clive Sansom

Nature he loves, and next to Nature – death,
When he deprives some creature of its breath
The man is happy in his joyless fashion;
For sport to him's a stern compulsive passion,
And in its service he devotes his leisure
Proving how grimly men can take their pleasure.

In better days, when maps were red, not Red,
He courted lions till those lions were dead;
Conducted, with a shrewd appraising eye,
Brisk love affairs with hippopotami;
And when he hunted tigers with a rajah
The ones he bagged were usually the larger.

Now, with the cost of living to enforce it,
Extermination is confined to Dorset.
He can't indulge his old romantic habits
And must content himself with potting rabbits –
Or pheasants, at a friend's estate near Sherborne,
So stuffed with corn as to be scarcely airborne.

But in his dreams voluptuous rhinos swim
And tigers roar their enormous love for him,
While he, with tenderly-selected slugs,
Converts them all to trophies or to rugs. . . .
To me the situation is ironic:
Thank God my love of Nature is platonic!

Bullfight in the Sun

Dannie Abse

*Shining angels are but the conscience of Man; the black bull
is all of breathing Spain, and the embroidered matador a
rich murderer. Angel of Europe, you did not intervene.*

The public matador in his arrogant yellow suit.
Olé, Olé,' they shout as he waves his red
advertisement for death. But I throw down a lonely
black tear of silence for the great black bull.

The intimate banderillos go home two after two.
Sacrifice on the sand and the sad horns going up
seeking hairless flesh. Fans click. The great black
bull oozes a tumour of blood. Roses and flies descend.

But I throw down a black tear mourning a private
bull-dream that is broken. Oh Abraham where is
the exhumed angel? Here is a lens once filled
with a panorama of grass and blue harmonies of sky.

I did not order this ritual: the neutral trumpet
announcing Isaac, the bandaged blind horses,
the clinical picador with his pole of nascent wounds,
the dark hot chemicals on the back of the bull.

Tonight in the electric restaurants with red wine,
with white bread they will serve on chromium trays
a striped still corpse. I throw down my English
anger. I throw down useless residues of silence.

Angel you did not intercede. Intimacy of death
is no more. I throw down my two long black tears.
Without tourniquet, scalpels, scissors or chloroform
the great black bull is dead, four legs in the air.

A Black Rabbit Dies for its Country

Gavin Ewart

Born in the lab, I never saw the grass
or felt the direct touch of wind or sun
and if a rabbit's nature is to run
free on the earth, I missed it; though the glass
never let shot or eager predators pass

while I was warm against my mother's side;
something was waiting in the centrifuge
(the world's a cage, although that cage is huge)
and separate I lived until I died —
watered and fed, I didn't fret, inside,

and all the time was waiting for the paste
scooped with a spatula from the metal rim,
and concentrate bacillus at the brim,
and lived the life of feeling and of taste.
I didn't know it. Knowing would be waste

in any case, and anthrax is the hard
stuff that knocks out the mice, the dogs, the men,
you haven't any chance at all and when
they've finished with you, you're down on a card.
How could I know, to be upon my guard

when they pushed my container into line
with the infected airstream? Breath is life;
though something there more deadly than the knife
cut into me, I was still feeling fine
and never guessed the next death would be mine

how many minutes later, lungs would choke
as feet beat out the seconds like a drum,
hands held me on the table, this was a sum
with the predicted ending of a joke.
Fighting I died, and no god even spoke.

The Island

J. C. Hall

It almost seemed they had waited a long age
For the wonder of our coming, the island birds,
And when we came, like children flocked around us,
Jostling and chattering, excited beyond words.

We had not expected a welcome such as this —
The curious tern peering into our faces,
The ceremonial bow of the albatross,
Flycatchers snatching our hair for their nesting places.

This was an alien world, locked out of time,
And we who had sailed there on the shifting winds,
What could we do but marvel? Such fearless breeds,
Such rare and impudent creatures charmed our minds.

67

We thought of the continents, our rank-rent homes,
Our children in piteous poverty, the wars
Of hunger and pride and power . . . Now it seemed
Forgotten Eden had opened wide its doors.

We stepped ashore amazed, then ferried over,
As from an ark, our chattels — a snorting band
Of cattle and randy goats. From the holds
The stowaway rats swarmed up and swam to land.

And all began . . . the ebony forests falling
To axe and mattock, centuries scorched away
At the touch of tinder, fabulous cargoes leaving
With our children's heritage, day after day.

Were we to blame, caught in such fierce endeavour,
That we never saw how we struck creation down —
The shimmering birdsong dying out at nightfall
Never to be reborn, grass turned to stone?

Were we to blame? We did not think so then,
But now we are driven out we know our blame.
On distant shores our fortunate kin await us.
When they jostle to greet us, how shall we hide our shame?

Nino, the Wonder Dog

Roy Fuller

A dog emerges from the flies
    Balanced upon a ball.
Our entertainment is the fear
    Or hope the dog will fall.

It comes and goes on larger spheres,
    And then walks on and halts
In the centre of the stage and turns
    Two or three somersaults.

The curtains descend upon the act.
    After a proper pause
The dog comes out between them to
    Receive its last applause.

Most mouths are set in pitying smiles,
  Few eyes are free from rheum:
The sensitive are filled with thoughts
  Of death and love and doom.

No doubt behind this ugly dog,
  Frail, fairly small, and white,
Stands some beneficent protector,
  Some life outside the night.

But this is not apparent as
  It goes, in the glare alone,
Through what it must to serve absurd-
  ities beyond its own.

Elephants in the Circus

D. H. Lawrence

Elephants in the circus
have aeons of weariness round their eyes.
Yet they sit up
and show vast bellies to the children.

The Leopards

Bernard Spencer

One of them was licking the bars of its circus-cage
then gazing out sleepily round the tall tent splendid
just here and there with scarlet and brass,
till the bang of a whip

Brought the animals lolloping on to their chairs (a tail
hung long and twitching, talking its own thoughts). Possibly
the threat was lies, it was not so much
the percussion

Of the whip, but instead some gipsy trick of the tents
won over those golden kittens to rise and beg
and flaunt their white, powder-puff bellies
(though at the report

69

Of a lash that curls too near, out flutters a paw
like a discharge from a fuse.)
                                        Now they were rolling
and cuddling with the bare-chest tamer;
now cowering at the whip-cut.

With humans one judges better; the tamed, the untamed.
It is harder with these pretenders — claws in, out,
— finally snaking off low to the ground:
yet there was a likeness, something stayed and haunted
as they bleared and snarled back over their narrow shoulders
at that whip banging.

Peacock

Judith Wright

Shame on the aldermen who locked
the Peacock in a dirty cage!
His blue and copper sheens are mocked
by habit, hopelessness and age.

The weary Sunday families
along their gravelled paths repeat
the pattern of monotonies
that he treads out with restless feet.

And yet the Peacock shines alone;
and if one metal feather fall
another grows where that was grown.
Love clothes him still, in spite of all.

How pure the hidden spring must rise
that time and custom cannot stain!
It speaks its joy again — again.
Perhaps the aldermen are wise.

Au Jardin des Plantes

John Wain

The gorilla lay on his back,
One hand cupped under his head,
Like a man.

Like a labouring man tired with work,
A strong man with his strength burnt away
In the toil of earning a living.

Only of course he was not tired out with work,
Merely with boredom; his terrible strength
All burnt away by prodigal idleness.

A thousand days, and then a thousand days,
Idleness licked away his beautiful strength
He having no need to earn a living.

It was all laid on, free of charge.
We maintained him, not for doing anything,
But for being what he was.

And so that Sunday morning he lay on his back,
Like a man, like a worn-out man,
One hand cupped under his terrible hard head.

Like a man, like a man,
One of those we maintain, not for doing anything,
But for being what they are.

A thousand days, and then a thousand days,
With everything laid on, free of charge,
They cup their heads in prodigal idleness.

The Jaguar

Ted Hughes

The apes yawn and adore their fleas in the sun.
The parrots shriek as if they were on fire, or strut
Like cheap tarts to attract the stroller with the nut.
Fatigued with indolence, tiger and lion

Lie still as the sun. The boa-constrictor's coil
Is a fossil. Cage after cage seems empty, or
Stinks of sleepers from the breathing straw.
It might be painted on a nursery wall.

But who runs like the rest past these arrives
At a cage where the crowd stands, stares, mesmerized,
As a child at a dream, at a jaguar hurrying enraged
Through prison darkness after the drills of his eyes

On a short fierce fuse. Not in boredom —
The eye satisfied to be blind in fire,
By the bang of blood in the brain deaf the ear —
He spins from the bars, but there's no cage to him

More than to the visionary his cell:
His stride is wildernesses of freedom:
The world rolls under the long thrust of his heel.
Over the cage floor the horizons come.